To the South Pole

Library of Congress Number: 78-26274

1 2 3 4 5 6 7 8 9 0 83 82 81 80 79

Printed and bound in the United States of America.

Library of Congress Cataloging in Publication Data

Frazier, Carla.
To the South Pole.

SUMMARY: Narrates the dangers and hardships faced by Roald Amundsen as he battled to be the first to overcome the difficulties of the journey to the South Pole.
1. Amundsen, Roald Engelbrecht Gravning, 1872-1928 — Juvenile literature. 2. Antarctic regions — Juvenile literature. 3. South Pole — Juvenile literature.
[1. South Pole. 2. Antarctic regions. 3. Amundsen, Roald Engelbrecht Gravning, 1872-1928] I. Manton, Dennis. II. Title.
G875.A48F72 919.8 [B] 78-26274
ISBN 0-8393-0153-7 lib. bdg.

To the South Pole

By
Carla Frazier

Illustrations by
Dennis Manton

Raintree Publishers
Milwaukee • Toronto • Melbourne • London

On January 14, 1911, Roald Amundsen and his companions reached the Barrier. Before them they saw a shining wall of ice that stretched across the Antarctic seas. This was their gateway to Antarctica, the coldest, highest, driest, and windiest continent on earth. A few explorers had explored the edges of Antarctica. Some had climbed the great volcano Mt. Erebus. But no one had ever reached the heart of the continent. No one has seen the very bottom of the world, the South Pole.

The ship *Fram* had sailed from Norway seven months before. It brought Amundsen, his companions, and sledge dogs into the Bay of Whales, and anchored along the Barrier.

Amundsen wanted to be the first person to reach the South Pole. So did Robert Scott, an Englishman who had landed with his men about 400 miles from Amundsen. Each explorer knew that the other was heading for the pole. The journey had become more than exploration for both men. It had become a race.

As soon as they landed, Amundsen and eight companions began to set up a base. They found a sheltered spot on the ice not far from the bay and raised tents. They called their base Framheim.

Amundsen's men carefully unloaded 900 cases of food and supplies from the *Fram.* They knew that when winter came the ice would close up and the *Fram* would leave. They would be on their own through the terrible Antarctic winter, waiting for the great trip in the spring.

By February they had established their base. Their next job before winter came was to set up supply stations along their intended route. When they began their journey to the pole, they wanted to have supplies waiting for them. Amundsen and three companions put on thick reindeer-skin clothing to protect them from the bitter cold. With three sleds loaded with supplies they set out toward the South Pole.

Despite a light fog, they covered the unknown ground fairly easily. In four days they reached the spot where they set up their first depot. They marked the spot and turned homeward. By the time they returned to Framheim, the *Fram* had sailed to avoid being trapped in the closing ice. The nine explorers were alone on the Barrier. If anything went wrong, they could not be rescued for months.

More stations had to be established. Eight men set out for the second trip.

With seven sleds and 42 dogs, the men carried a huge store of supplies. They were too confident. The temperature was far below zero. The heavy loads began to tire the dogs. They passed the first supply station and set up a second one farther south. Still they pushed on toward the pole. Now they were traveling across ice where ridges and cracks made the journey slow and dangerous. Although most of Antarctica is covered with ice thousands of feet thick, that ice is not solid. It is cut through with deep crevasses that are hard to see. Ice that seems to be solid can turn out to be only a shell over a deep chasm. As the men and dogs made their way across this dangerous land, the three leading dogs disappeared. They had fallen into one of the deep crevasses that crisscrossed the route. Luckily the dogs were held by their harnesses, and they were pulled safely to the surface. The ice had given warning of its treacherous nature.

Despite the terrible conditions, the party set up a third station, but they could go no further. The bitter cold and the wind were taking their toll. The dogs were beginning to die of cold and exhaustion. They had to turn back. Eight dogs had died by the time they got back to Framheim.

The days became shorter and shorter until the sun no longer rose above the horizon. The Antarctic winter had begun.

The men kept busy through the long, dark winter by caring for the dogs and making preparations for their journey. They made the sleds as light as possible. They tunneled through the snow to make extra rooms. Their clothing was made to protect them from the dangers of frostbite and snow blindness. They checked and packed their food and equipment.

The days began to get longer. By September 8, spring seemed to have arrived. The men were impatient to start again.

At last Amundsen led his men south. After resting all winter, the dogs were wild and unwilling to work. But at the back of everyone's mind was the thought that Scott and his men might already be on their way to the pole.

After they set out, the Antarctic weather turned against them. The temperature, which had been rising, dropped well below zero. Their feet began to freeze. Amundsen decided to abandon the journey, and the party returned to Framheim, temporarily defeated.

On October 19, Amundsen started out again. This time he was determined to reach the pole. He took with him just four men on skis and four sleds, each drawn by thirteen dogs. The weather stayed mild. They moved quickly, picking up supplies at the three stations they had fought so hard to establish.

After they passed the third station, they were on unknown ground. They made their way toward a far-off mountain range, setting up more stations as they went. Once a sled dropped over the edge of a crevasse. The men and dogs struggled to hold on to it. Finally, one of the men climbed over the edge on a rope to help get it back. He saw that the ice they all stood on was only a few inches thick. They pulled up the sled and moved away quickly, knowing that danger lay all around them.

Soon they reached a great glacier that ran between some mountains. It would be difficult and dangerous to climb, but it led to the pole. Amundsen and his men were determined to conquer it.

The dogs worked hard on the steep climb. The men pushed, pulled, and coaxed the dogs until at last they reached a place where they could camp. Here Amundsen and his men had to perform a terrible task. They could not take all their dogs with them to the pole. Only eighteen were needed. So with sorrow in their hearts, the explorers killed the extra animals. The dogs had done their best, but they were killed and their flesh was used to feed the other dogs. The howl of the wind surrounded them.

They continued their journey in a blizzard that blinded them. Another glacier reared up ahead of them. It was pitted with huge crevasses that could swallow them all if they took one careless step.

Amundsen led his party over thin bridges of snow. They climbed around vast blocks of ice and over slippery ridges that blocked their path. It took all their courage and skill to conquer the "Devil's Glacier," as they named it.

As they struggled onward they wondered about the English explorer Scott. How near was he to the pole? Scott didn't trust dogs for this work. His men were using ponies and their own muscles to pull their sleds. Were ponies really better? Would Scott reach the pole ahead of Amundsen?

A high ridge blocked Amundsen's way, but they got through a narrow gap called Hell's Gate and on to the "Devil's Ballroom." They were now crossing a slippery layer of ice so thin that their footsteps made hollow echoes as they walked. A little way below was another layer of ice that they thought was solid. Suddenly the lead man, Bjaaland, fell through the ice! At the last minute, he grabbed onto some rope from his sled. Only his quick reactions saved Bjaaland from certain death.

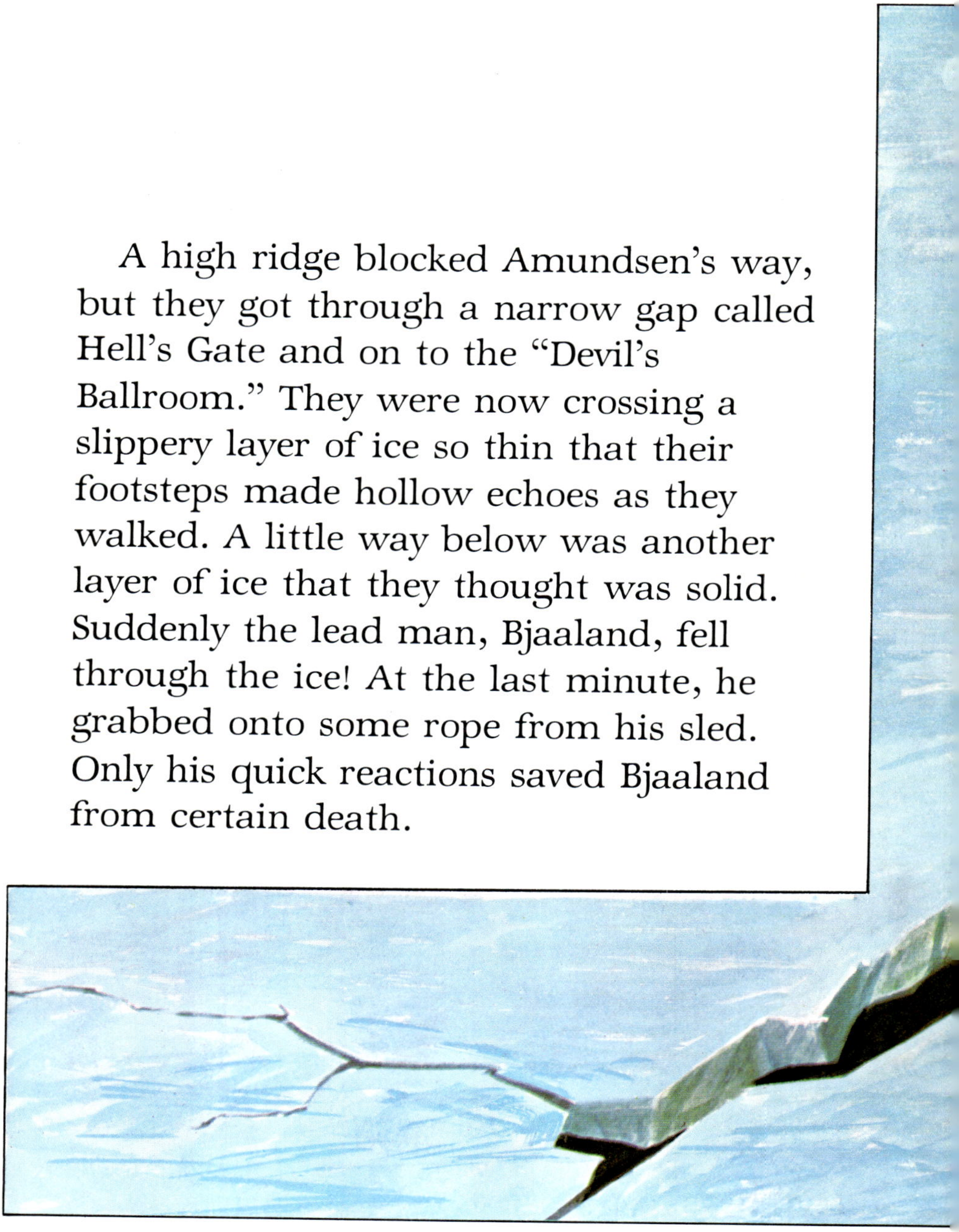

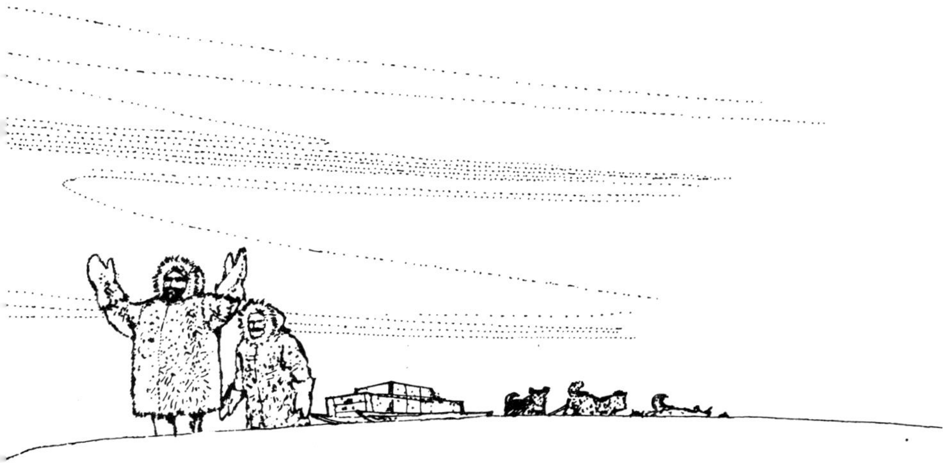

At last they reached the polar plateau. Greatly encouraged, Amundsen led the way forward. He was stopped by a joyful shout from his companions, who were all looking at their compasses. They had passed the point reached by the English explorer Shackleton. They had now journeyed further south than anyone had before them. It was a wonderful moment. As they unfurled the Norwegian flag, Amundsen had tears in his eyes.

It now seemed certain that they would reach their goal, but one fear haunted them. What if the British team led by Captain Scott had already reached the pole?

On December 13, they knew they were near the pole. Amundsen kept waking that night, feeling, in his words, like "a little boy on the night before Christmas eve." On the afternoon of the next day, December 14, 1911, Amundsen and his companions checked their compasses. They had reached the South Pole. Around them stretched a bleak, forbidding plain of ice. Together the five men solemnly planted the Norwegian flag. The ground was unmarked, and they knew they were the first to stand on that spot. They had won the race to the pole. It was a day that would be remembered in history.

Amundsen returned to Framheim on January 25, 1912. He had been gone for 98 days and had covered 1,860 miles. The men were exhausted and their skins ravaged by frostbite. Only 11 of their dogs had survived. With joy, Amundsen's party greeted their companions at the base. The next day they gave the news of their victory to the crew of the *Fram*, which had returned to collect the explorers.

Antarctica was not so kind to Scott and his companions. On their disappointed way back from the pole they ran into terrible blizzards. They died a few miles from safety.

Her decks draped with flags, the *Fram* sailed out of the Bay of Whales on January 30. Amundsen turned for one last look at the expanse of ice and snow that had been his home for more than a year. The Barrier was shrouded in fog. Antarctica was hidden from the man who had conquered it and won his way to the South Pole.